Turnaround: How God Can Take You from Setback to Comeback

Copyright © 2025 Joel Osteen

All rights reserved. No part of this book may be reproduced or transmitted in any form or by any means, electronic or mechanical, including photocopying, recording, or by any information storage and retrieval system, without permission in writing from the publisher.

Scripture quotations marked ESV are taken from The ESV® Bible (The Holy Bible, English Standard Version®), © 2001 by Crossway, a publishing ministry of Good News Publishers. Used by permission. All rights reserved.

Scripture quotations marked MSG are taken from *The Message*, copyright © 1993, 2002, 2018 by Eugene H. Peterson. Used by permission of NavPress. All rights reserved. Represented by Tyndale House Publishers.

Scripture quotations marked NIV are taken from the Holy Bible, New International Version®, NIV®. Copyright © 1973, 1978, 1984, 2011 by Biblica, Inc. Used by permission of Zondervan. All rights reserved worldwide. www.zondervan.com.

Scripture quotations marked NKJV are taken from the New King James Version®. Copyright © 1982 by Thomas Nelson. Used by permission. All rights reserved.

Scripture quotations marked NLT are taken from the *Holy Bible*, New Living Translation, copyright © 1996, 2004, 2015 by Tyndale House Foundation. Used by permission of Tyndale House Publishers, Carol Stream, Illinois 60188. All rights reserved.

ISBN: 978-1-963492-37-8

Created and assembled for Joel Osteen Ministries by
Breakfast for Seven
breakfastforseven.com

Printed in the United States of America.

For additional resources by Joel Osteen, visit JoelOsteen.com.

TURN-AROUND

How God Can Take You from Setback to Comeback

Joel Osteen

Table of Contents

INTRODUCTION

CHAPTER 1
**THE PROMISE
WILL BE FULFILLED** 1

CHAPTER 2
**FROM A PIT
TO YOUR PURPOSE** 13

CHAPTER 3
**THE SEA
WILL PART** 25

CHAPTER 4
**YOUR WAITING
IS NEVER WASTED** 37

CHAPTER 5
**THE BATTLE
IS ALREADY WON** 49

CHAPTER 6
**PROVISION IN
THE IMPROBABLE** 61

CHAPTER 7
**REACH
FOR YOUR HEALING** 73

CHAPTER 8
**BELIEF THAT
BREAKS BARRIERS** 85

CHAPTER 9
**GRACE
IS GREATER** 97

CHAPTER 10
**A FAITH-FILLED
FOCUS** 109

CHAPTER 11
**RETURN
AND REJOICE** 121

CHAPTER 12
**WORSHIP THAT
BREAKS THROUGH** 133

Introduction

Turnaround.

I want that word to resound in your spirit. Let it anchor your heart. No matter what you're facing, no matter how impossible it seems . . .

God can turn the situation around for your good.

You may be in a season where you feel stuck, where the answers aren't coming, where hope feels far away.

God hasn't forgotten you.

Perhaps picking up this book felt foolish. You want to have hope, but you question its reality when all you see and feel is hope-less.

A turnaround is coming. Your story isn't over.

Throughout Scripture, we see people like you and me who faced overwhelming circumstances. People who waited years to see a promise fulfilled. People who failed, felt outnumbered, overlooked, and wondered if they were disqualified from God's blessing.

In every story, however, we also find something remarkable, something I love to refer to as a "faith turnaround point" — a moment when a person courageously chose to believe God's promise would come to pass. A moment when the Almighty stepped in and did what no one thought was possible.

God hasn't changed. What He did then, He can do for you now!

Maybe you're believing for a miracle. Perhaps you're holding on for a breakthrough in your health, your relationships, your finances, or your dreams. Maybe you're just trying to get through the day, wondering if things will ever get better.

This book is for you. And I believe and declare that as you read every page, this declaration will become more than a prayer but your reality:

God is bringing a turnaround to your life!

Chapter 1

THE PROMISE WILL BE FULFILLED

We who have run for our very lives to God have every reason to grab the promised hope with both hands and never let go.

HEBREWS 6:18 (MSG)

We find Abraham and Sarah's story in the book of Genesis.

For years, they longed for a child. They had a promise from God that they would be the parents of many nations. But as the years went by, Sarah didn't get pregnant, and their hope began to fade. She became well past childbearing age, and everything in the natural said it was too late.

But just when it seemed impossible, God reaffirmed His word . . .

> *"Is anything too hard for the LORD? I will return to you at the appointed time next year, and Sarah shall have a son."*
> Genesis 18:14 (NIV)

Your
FAITH TURN-AROUND POINT

Even when it doesn't make sense, keep trusting God because His promises never fail!

Maybe there's a dream in your heart that feels like it will never happen.

Maybe you've been waiting, praying, believing — but nothing seems to be changing. You're wondering if you should give up, if it's too late, if you missed your moment.

Let me encourage you . . .

> **Nothing is too hard for the Lord! Just because you don't see anything happening doesn't mean God isn't working. Your promise is already scheduled and will be fulfilled!**

Abraham and Sarah didn't see God at work for years.

When God first called Abraham (then Abram), he was seventy-five years old. Sarah was sixty-five. They had no children, yet God gave them a radical promise — that Abraham would become the father of many nations (Genesis 17:5).

God wants to step into your impossibility and remind you that nothing is too hard for Him.

At first, they believed. They held on to hope. But as the years passed, nothing happened. And in their culture, barrenness wasn't just disappointing — it was considered shameful. It made a woman feel like she had no worth.

At one point, Sarah took matters into her own hands. She told Abraham to have a child with her servant, Hagar. It seemed the only logical way to fulfill the promise. Ishmael was born, but this wasn't God's plan.

By the time Abraham was 99 and Sarah was 89, they had given up. It was biologically impossible. That's when God appeared to Abraham again and reaffirmed His promise:

> *"Is anything too hard for the LORD? I will return to you at the appointed time next year, and Sarah shall have a son."*

Sarah overheard and laughed. Not out of joy — but disbelief. How could this happen now, when it hadn't happened for decades? But God asked a question that changed everything, and I encourage you to ask it as well: *"Is anything too hard for the Lord?"*

God wants to step into your impossibility and remind you that nothing is too hard for him.

I wonder if that's a question you need to declare over a circumstance or situation in your life . . .

Have you been praying for years for a loved one to come back to faith? *Is anything too hard for the Lord?*

Are you struggling in your marriage, wondering if restoration is possible? *Is anything too hard for the Lord?*

Does your financial situation look hopeless? *Is anything too hard for the Lord?*

Are you facing a dire medical diagnosis? *Is anything too hard for the Lord?*

Do you feel like your dreams have passed you by? *Is anything too hard for the Lord?*

Does it feel like your prayers aren't making a difference? *Is anything too hard for the Lord?*

Are you carrying the weight of anxiety or fear about the future? *Is anything too hard for the Lord?*

Are you exhausted from waiting for a breakthrough, for a promise from God to be fulfilled? *Is anything too hard for the Lord?*

Just like Abraham and Sarah, you're going to laugh again. You're going to hope again. You're going to see the faithfulness of God in your life.

Your Heavenly Father's timing is perfect. His power is limitless. Luke 1:37 declares, *"For with God nothing will be impossible"* (NKJV).

When Isaac was born, a woman who had been barren for 90 years held a son in her arms. Romans 4:18 says, *"Against all hope, Abraham in hope believed and so became the father of many nations"* (NIV). He saw the promise come to pass.

But their story was always about more than receiving a child — it was about discovering God is never late, never limited, and never unable to fulfill His promises. And if He did it for Abraham and Sarah, He can do it for you!

The author of Hebrews wrote:

> *When God made his promise to Abraham, he backed it all the way, putting his own reputation on the line. He said,* **"I promise that I'll bless you with everything I have — bless and bless and bless!"** *Abraham stuck it out and got everything that had been promised to him.*

*When people make promises, they guarantee them by appeal to some authority above them so that if there is any question that they'll make good on the promise, the authority will back them up. When God wanted to guarantee his promises, he gave his word, a rock-solid guarantee — **God can't break his word**. And because his word cannot change, the promise is likewise unchangeable.*

We who have run for our very lives to God have every reason to grab the promised hope with both hands and never let go. *It's an unbreakable spiritual lifeline, reaching past all appearances right to the very presence of God where Jesus, running on ahead of us, has taken up his permanent post as high priest for us, in the order of Melchizedek.* Hebrews 6:13–20 (MSG, emphasis added)

Against all hope, Abraham in hope believed and so became the father of many nations.

ROMANS 4:18 (NIV)

And we know that God causes everything to work together for the good of those who love God and are called according to his purpose for them.

ROMANS 8:28 (NLT, EMPHASIS ADDED)

Joseph had big dreams — visions from God that foretold greatness in his future. But after years of betrayal, injustice, and imprisonment, his destiny seemed lost.

Forgotten and alone, Joseph surely wondered when his situation would change. All the while, God was setting him up for a turnaround . . .

> *Then Pharaoh sent and called Joseph, and they quickly brought him out of the pit.*
> Genesis 41:14 (ESV)

Your
FAITH
TURN-
AROUND
POINT

Choose to see every setback as a setup — God is positioning you for something greater!

In one moment, Joseph's entire life shifted. He woke up a prisoner, but by the end of the day, he was standing before Pharaoh.

The waiting season was over — his breakthrough had arrived!

God did more than deliver Joseph — He positioned him for favor.

He turned every setback into a setup for something better. And He wants to do the same in your life and for your purpose!

Joseph's story didn't start in a palace. It started in a pit, and not even the pit of a prison.

Years prior, his brothers were envious of him. Their father, Jacob, favored Joseph. And when Joseph shared a couple of dreams that set him as a ruler over them, it was the last straw. They schemed together, threw him into a pit, and then sold him into slavery.

Even as a slave, however, Joseph excelled. In the house of Potiphar, everything he touched was blessed.

> **God knows how to bring you out of the pit. When the time is right, He can shift everything in your favor in a moment.**

Unfortunately, Potiphar's wife noticed Joseph, and when he refused her advances, she falsely accused him and had him thrown into prison.

Joseph remained there for years. It looked like he was forgotten. But what Joseph didn't realize was that God was orchestrating everything behind the scenes.

Even at his lowest point, God still worked through him. He helped interpret dreams for others without receiving anything in return.

One day, Pharaoh had a dream no one could interpret. Suddenly, Joseph was remembered. He was called up, cleaned up, and taken straight to Pharaoh's court. With God's wisdom, Joseph interpreted the dream and gave Pharaoh a strategy to save Egypt from famine.

> **Just like that, Joseph went from the prison to the palace in a single day.**

You may wake up one morning feeling stuck, but by the end of the day, God can open a door you never saw coming.

Pharaoh was so impressed that he made Joseph second-in-command over Egypt. The very dream Joseph had all those years ago — of being in a place of leadership — would finally come to pass!

Time after time, God took what was meant for harm and used it to launch Joseph into his destiny. And not only did Joseph step into his dream, but he also saved countless lives, including his own family.

Maybe you feel like Joseph — you've been waiting, struggling, and feeling forgotten. You've been faithful, but nothing seems to be changing.

Let me encourage you — God knows how to bring you out of the pit. When the time is right, He can shift everything in your favor in a moment.

> **You may wake up one morning feeling stuck, but by the end of the day, God can open a door you never saw coming.**

He knows how to put your name in the right places, bring the right connections, and take you from obscurity to influence.

Don't give up on your dreams if it's taking longer than you expected. You are not forgotten! Like Joseph, God is setting you up for something better. Stay faithful, stay ready, and trust that when the appointed time comes, He will bring you out *quickly*.

Your breakthrough is closer than you think, and your purpose will be fulfilled!

"You intended to harm me, but God intended it all for good. He brought me to this position so I could save the lives of many people."

GENESIS 50:20 (NLT, EMPHASIS ADDED)

Chapter 3
THE SEA WILL PART

"In your unfailing love you will lead the people you have redeemed. In your strength you will guide them to your holy dwelling."

EXODUS 15:13 (NIV)

Let me set the scene. The Israelites have been freed from slavery in Egypt. After centuries of oppression, God performed miracle after miracle on their behalf.

But as quickly as they escaped, they found themselves trapped — Pharaoh's army closing in behind them, and the Red Sea stretched out before them.

There was no way forward and no way back. Afraid for their lives, they cried out to Moses, *"Why did you bring us out here to die in the wilderness?"* (Exodus 14:11, NLT). What they didn't know was that God was about to turn it around for their good . . .

> *And Moses said to the people, "Do not be afraid. Stand still, and see the salvation of the LORD, which He will accomplish for you today. For the Egyptians whom you see today, you shall see again no more forever. The LORD will fight for you, and you shall hold your peace." And the LORD said to Moses, "Why do you cry to Me? Tell the children of Israel to go forward."*
> Exodus 14:13–15 (NKJV)

Your FAITH TURN-AROUND POINT

In the face of fear, keep moving forward in faith. God is making a way!

The Israelites were in full panic mode.

The enemy was closing in, and they saw no escape. But Moses stood up and declared, "Stand firm. Watch what God is about to do."

Then, God gave a command to Moses: "Raise your staff. Stretch out your hand over the sea. Go forward!"

When Moses obeyed, the waters parted. A massive highway formed right through the middle of the sea!

The Israelites walked across on dry ground. And when Pharaoh's army tried to follow, the waters came crashing down, destroying the enemy completely.

What seemed like a trap was a divine setting for victory.

But here's what's important to realize: God wasn't asking the Israelites to figure it out — He was asking them to trust Him.

The same God who parted the Red Sea *then* is the same God who is making a way for you *now*. Keep moving forward in faith!

In the natural, there was no escape. But God isn't limited by the natural. He didn't need a bridge. He didn't need boats. He simply parted the waters.

The same sea that seemed like an obstacle became the very thing that brought Israel freedom, blessing, and victory.

Maybe right now you feel like the Israelites — you're up against something impossible. You don't see a way forward. The enemy is closing in. You feel stuck.

Perhaps you thought your marriage or another relationship in your life was strong, but things have taken a turn for the worse. It looks beyond repair.

Instead of ending in ruin, God wants to step in, soften hearts, bring reconciliation, and strengthen the relationship in ways you never imagined.

Watch what God is about to do and keep moving forward in faith.

Maybe you've worked hard, but you keep hitting a ceiling. A promotion went to someone else. A door you were sure would open slammed shut. It feels like you're stuck.

Nevertheless, God isn't limited by human decisions.

In an instant, a breakthrough can appear — a job you never applied for, an unexpected victory, or favor that restores a relationship.

You don't have to figure out a solution. Simply trust God where you are. He didn't bring you this far to leave you.

He's already working behind the scenes, lining up the right opportunities, the right connections, and the right breakthroughs.

> **When you feel overwhelmed, do what Moses said: Stand firm. Be still. Watch what God is about to do and keep moving forward in faith.**

Your Red Sea is about to part! What looks like a dead end is about to turn into a supernatural breakthrough.

The same God who made a way for the Israelites is making a way for you now.

"With your unfailing love you lead the people you have redeemed. In your might, you guide them to your sacred home. . . . You will bring them in and plant them on your own mountain — the place, O LORD, reserved for your own dwelling, the sanctuary, O LORD, that your hands have established. The LORD will reign forever and ever!"

EXODUS 15:13, 17–18 (NLT)

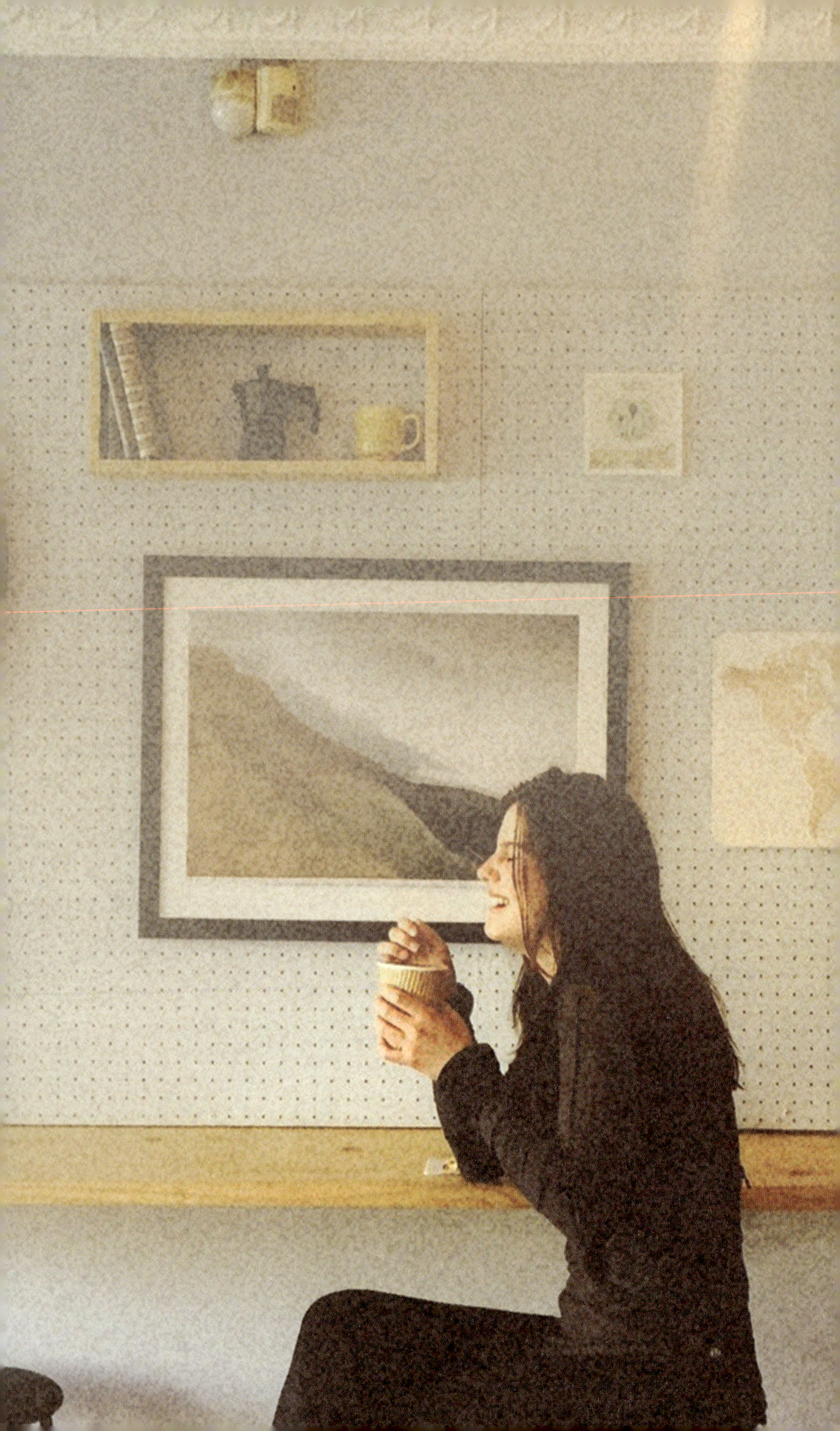

Chapter 4

YOUR WAITING IS NEVER WASTED

"My heart rejoices in the LORD! The LORD has made me strong. Now I have an answer for my enemies; I rejoice because you rescued me. No one is holy like the LORD! There is no one besides you; there is no Rock like our God."

1 SAMUEL 2:1-2 (NLT)

We find Hannah in 1 Samuel 1. She longed for a child. Year after year, she prayed and believed, yet nothing changed. To make matters worse, she was constantly reminded of her barrenness by Peninnah, her husband's other wife, who had children and made sure Hannah felt the weight of her disappointment.

It seemed like God was silent. Her prayers went unanswered. But what Hannah didn't realize was that God was setting her up for something greater than she ever imagined . . .

> *"Go in peace, and may the God of Israel grant you what you have asked of him."*
> 1 Samuel 1:17 (NIV)

Your FAITH TURN- AROUND POINT

Choose to see delay not as denial but as divine preparation and positioning by God!

One day, Hannah was at the temple, pouring her heart out to God. She was so desperate and full of emotion that the priest, Eli, thought she was drunk (1 Samuel 1:14).

He saw her pouring her heart out to God in prayer, asking for children. But instead of rebuking her, Eli spoke a word over her: *"Go in peace, and may the God of Israel grant you what you have asked of him"* (1 Samuel 1:17, NIV).

Something inside Hannah shifted. She wasn't pregnant yet, but she received that word in her spirit. She wiped her tears, left the temple, and Scripture says she was no longer downcast (v. 18).

Soon after, she conceived and gave birth to a son — Samuel. Not just any child, but a prophet of God, one who would anoint kings and change the course of history.

Hannah wanted a son — God gave her a legacy.

He took her years of pain and turned them into a testimony of faith. He used what seemed like a delay to bring about one of the greatest prophets in Israel's history.

The delay isn't God's denial. It's divine positioning. Your answer is already on the way!

If Hannah had received a child earlier, she might not have dedicated him to God. But because of her journey, she made a vow — Samuel would belong to the Lord.

The delay was never denial. It was divine positioning.

Maybe you've been waiting on a promise from God. You've prayed, you've believed, but nothing seems to be happening.

Let me encourage you:

Just because it's taking time doesn't mean God isn't working!

You might feel like Hannah — waiting, longing, wondering when your breakthrough will come. *What if your delay is God setting you up for more than you imagined?*

What if the job you're praying for is still being prepared? The connections, the promotion, the opportunity — God is aligning every detail.

What if God isn't only answering your prayer — He's positioning you for a testimony?

What if the relationship you've been waiting for needs time to grow into what God wants it to be?

What if the dream in your heart is even bigger than you think? What if God isn't only answering your prayer — He's positioning you for a testimony?

Hannah walked away from the temple in faith. She left before she saw the miracle, but she believed it was on the way.

That's the kind of faith God honors.

Hannah could have given up. She could have gotten bitter. But instead, she kept pressing in. She kept believing. She kept praying. And at the right time, God showed up.

If you're in a season of waiting, don't lose heart. Your answer is already on the way. God hasn't forgotten you. He's heard your every prayer, seen your every tear, and He is working behind the scenes on your behalf.

Like Hannah, choose to believe it before you see it. Shift your mindset.

Wipe your tears. Start expecting again!

Second Corinthians 1:20 (NLT) says, *"For all of God's promises have been fulfilled in Christ with a resounding 'Yes!' And through Christ, our 'Amen' (which means 'Yes') ascends to God for his glory."*

The delay isn't denial. Your miracle is closer than you think!

"As surely as you live, I am the woman who stood here beside you praying to the LORD. I prayed for this child, and the LORD has granted me what I asked of him. So now I give him to the LORD."

1 SAMUEL 1:26-28 (NIV)

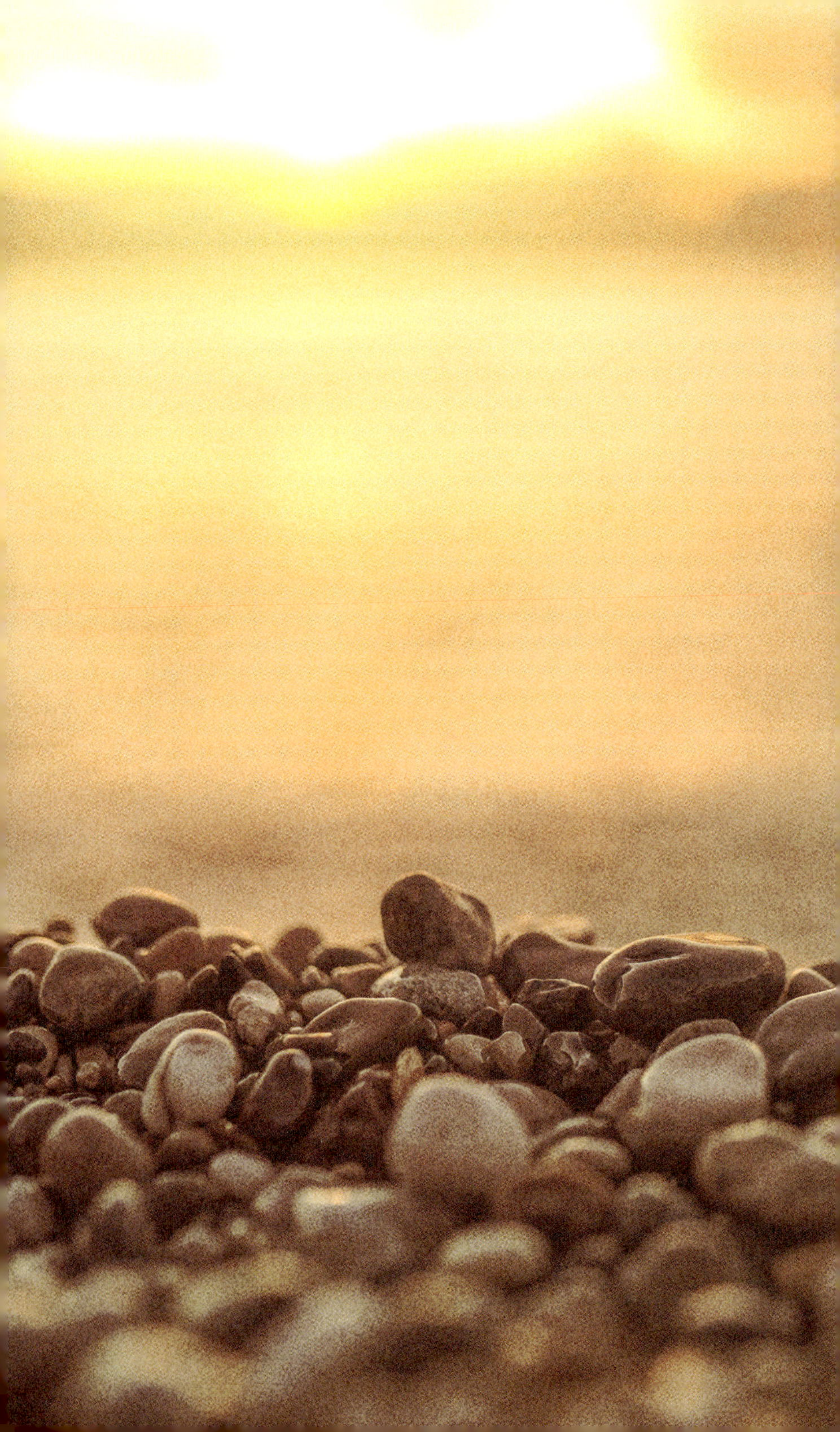

Chapter 5

THE BATTLE IS ALREADY WON

"The LORD who rescued me from the paw of the lion and the paw of the bear will rescue me from the hand of this Philistine."

1 SAMUEL 17:37 (NIV)

THE BATTLE IS ALREADY WON

The Israelites were terrified. Every morning and evening, for 40 days, a giant named Goliath from the Philistine army stepped onto the battlefield at the Valley of Elah, taunting them, challenging them, and daring anyone to fight him.

No one had the courage to step forward. Then along came David — a young shepherd boy. Too small to wear armor. Too inexperienced to be taken seriously. But while everyone else saw an unbeatable giant, David saw an opportunity for God to show His power . . .

> *"You come against me with sword and spear and javelin, but I come against you in the name of the LORD Almighty, the God of the armies of Israel, whom you have defied."*
> 1 Samuel 17:45 (NIV)

Your

FAITH TURN-AROUND POINT

Shift your focus from the size of your obstacle to the greatness of your God.

The rest of Israel saw an enemy too big to defeat. David saw an enemy too big to miss.

Israel saw a giant too powerful to overcome. David saw a giant who was powerless compared to the strength of his God.

Israel saw their own weakness. David saw a divine turnaround.

Today, you may be standing in front of a giant. It looks impossible. It feels overwhelming. The enemy wants you to believe you're outmatched, that you don't have what it takes, and that the battle is already lost.

But what do you see?

Do you see an impossible situation — or a setup for God's power to be revealed?

The obstacles that once seemed too big can turn into pebbles that pave the path to your future!

Do you see yourself as weak and unqualified — or as someone anointed, appointed, and equipped by the Most High God?

Do you see an obstacle too big to move — or a problem God is more than able to overcome?

When Goliath mocked David, David didn't back down. He declared the victory before it even happened. He ran toward the giant, slung a single stone, and watched as Goliath fell to the ground.

No sword. No armor. No army. Just faith in the power of God.

And here's the thing: even though the victory was massive for David and the nation of Israel at the time, David was still being prepared for something greater.

This story wasn't just about Goliath. What seemed like an impossible challenge was actually the doorway to his future as king.

Likewise, the battle you're facing is about more than this moment — it's about your destiny. And when you step out like David — when you trust God completely — you're going to see your giants fall.

The obstacles that once seemed too big can turn into pebbles that pave the path to your future!

- If you have a big presentation at work, don't choose fear but faith in God. Prepare diligently, stand up confidently, and speak with authority.

- If you have a conflict with a loved one, don't choose pride but humility before God and others. Speak the truth in love and be quicker to listen than to get angry.

- If you're facing a financial struggle, don't choose worry but trust in God's provision. Be a good steward, remain generous, and believe that He will meet your needs.

- If you're battling insecurity, don't choose comparison but confidence in who God made you to be. Focus on His calling for your life and walk boldly in your unique purpose.

- If you're facing rejection, don't choose bitterness but rest in God's acceptance. Remember that your worth isn't based on others' opinions but on His unfailing love.

God performed the miracle, but David knew how to sling a stone.

Faith isn't passive — it partners with preparation.

David had already confronted and overcome a lion and a bear with that same sling.

What seemed like ordinary battles in the pasture was God training him for a greater victory. So, when the pasture turned into a battlefield, David was ready. He didn't wait for the giant to fall on his own; he stepped forward, used what he had, and trusted God with the outcome.

As you do the same, the obstacles — the "giants" — that once seemed big will turn into pebbles that pave the path to your future, in Jesus' name!

Now this I know: The LORD gives victory to his anointed. He answers him from his heavenly sanctuary with the victorious power of his right hand. Some trust in chariots and some in horses, but we trust in the name of the LORD our God. They are brought to their knees and fall, but we rise up and stand firm.

PSALM 20:6-8 (NIV)

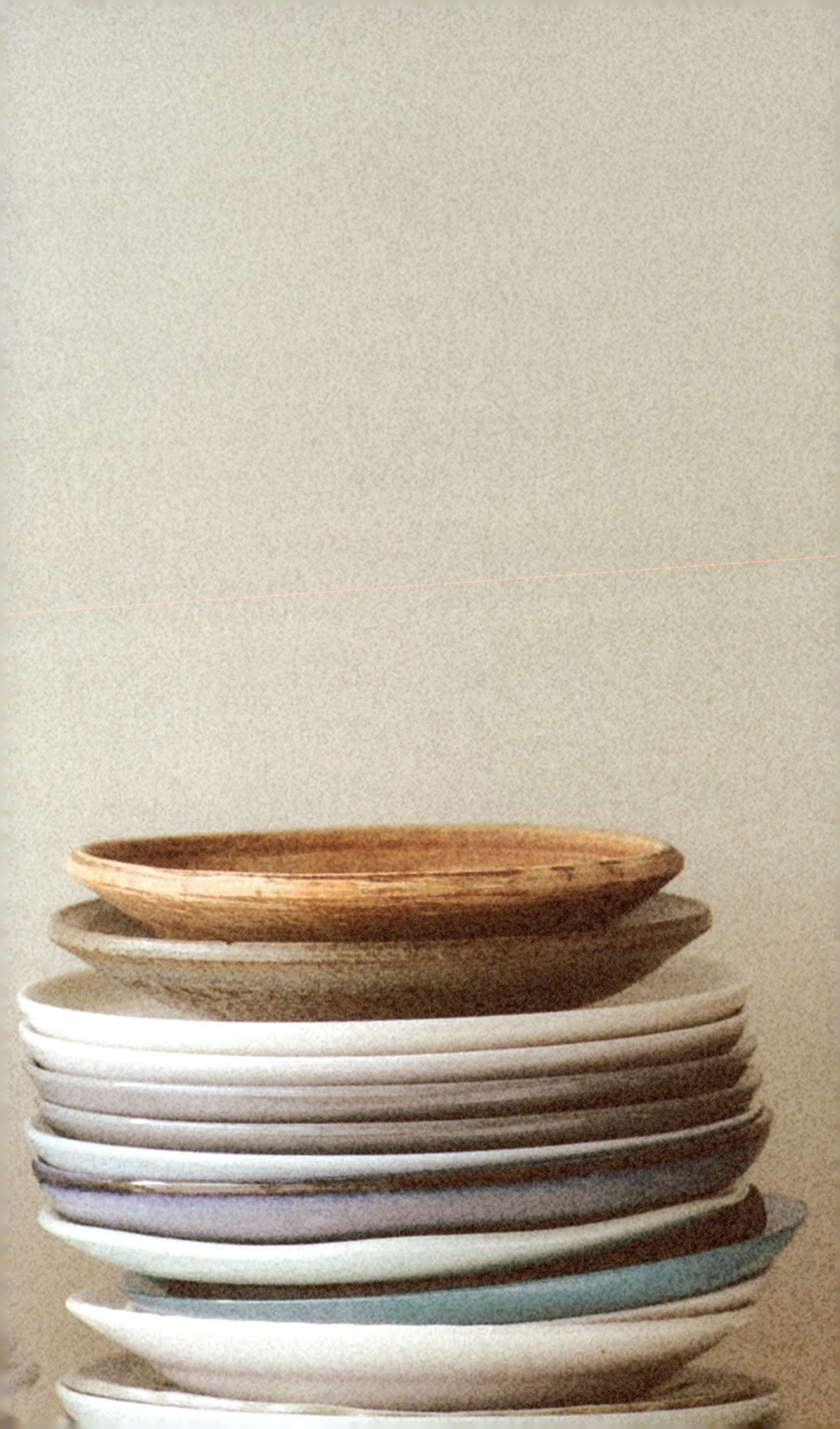

Chapter 6

PROVISION IN THE IMPROBABLE

For the jar of flour was not used up and the jug of oil did not run dry, in keeping with the word of the LORD spoken by Elijah.

1 KINGS 17:16 (NIV)

A severe drought struck the land of Israel. Crops had dried, food was scarce, and people were struggling to survive. In the middle of it all was a widow — alone, with barely enough flour and oil to make a final meal for herself and her son.

Suddenly, a prophet named Elijah showed up. He asked her for water and food, but she told him, "I only have enough for one last meal. Then we will die."

It seemed like a callous and cruel request from the prophet. But what she didn't realize was that God was about to turn her lack into abundance . . .

> *"For this is what the* Lord, *the God of Israel, says: 'The jar of flour will not be used up and the jug of oil will not run dry until the day the* Lord *sends rain on the land.'"*
> 1 Kings 17:14 (NIV)

Your
FAITH TURN-AROUND POINT

Boldly step out in obedience to God's Word — provision flows when faith is put into action!

Elijah told the widow to make him a small loaf of bread *first*, then to prepare something for herself and her son.

She had a choice — hold on to what little she had or trust God's word.

Courageously, she took a step of faith. She used the last of her flour and oil to make that small loaf for Elijah. Then something miraculous happened — her jar of flour never ran out and her jug of oil never went dry.

Every day, there was enough. God sustained her and her son, not just for a day, but for the entire duration of the drought!

God didn't merely provide for her needs — He multiplied what she thought wasn't enough.

She was preparing for death when God was about to display His faithfulness. And notice, He didn't give her a full pantry overnight — He gave her a daily supply.

Maybe today, you feel like this widow. You're running on empty. You don't see how you're going to make it.

> **God can take what little you have, or even what you think is lost, and multiply it beyond what you imagined!**

Maybe it's your finances, your strength, or your hope — you feel like you have nothing left.

Let me remind you:

> **God is your provider. He is your source. He can take what little you have and multiply it beyond what you imagined!**

The key is to boldly trust God and be obedient to His Word, even when it doesn't make sense.

I mention that because the widow's story doesn't actually end with a miraculous jar of flour and jug of oil.

Sometime later, this woman's son got sick. Scripture says he got worse and worse until he finally stopped breathing (1 Kings 17:17).

The woman was heartbroken and disillusioned. After all, she had seen God's miraculous provision. She had trusted

God is your provider. He is your source. He can take what little you have and multiply it beyond what you imagined!

Him with her last meal, and He had sustained her and her son through a drought.

But now, her child — the very reason she had fought to survive — was gone.

The miracle she had clung to now felt like a cruel trick. Her grief turned into confusion, even blame. She cried out to Elijah, *"Did you come to remind me of my sin and kill my son?"* (1 Kings 17:18, NIV).

Have you ever felt that way?

You've seen God move; you've experienced His faithfulness, but suddenly, another crisis comes. You think . . .

God, I thought You were making a way! Why is this happening now?

Friend, just as God wasn't finished with the widow, He isn't finished with you.

Elijah took the boy and prayed for God to breathe life back into him. And God answered . . .

The boy's life returned, and the widow declared, *"Now I know that you are a man of God and that the word of the* Lord *from your mouth is the truth"* (v. 24).

> **God isn't only the God of "enough" — He is the God of restoration, resurrection, and more than enough.**

It may not come all at once, but you're not going under. God has a way to sustain you, keep you, and bless you.

Get ready — your jar of flour won't run out. Your oil won't dry up. God is about to bring supernatural provision into your life!

**The LORD is
my shepherd,
I lack nothing.**

PSALM 23:1 (NIV)

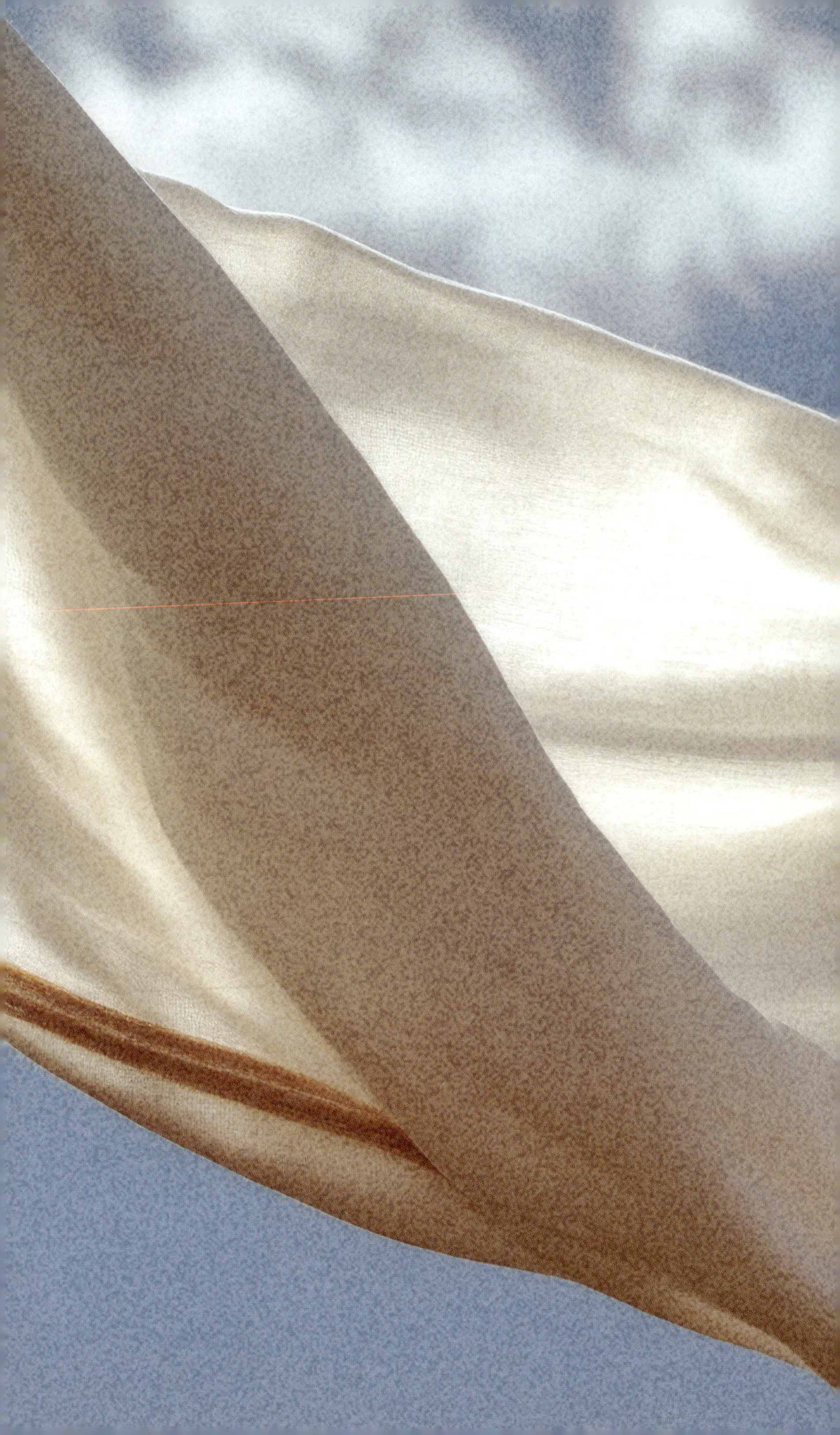

Chapter 7

REACH FOR YOUR HEALING

Jesus said to her, "Daughter, you took a risk of faith, and now you're healed and whole. Live well, live blessed! Be healed of your plague."

MARK 5:34 (MSG)

We find a faith-filled woman in Mark 5 who suffered for 12 long years. She had a condition that caused her to bleed continuously — something that was painful and humiliating.

According to Jewish law, she was considered unclean and had to remain isolated until the bleeding stopped. Rejected and out of options — she spent everything she had on doctors. But instead of getting better, she only got worse.

This woman had every reason to give up, but then she heard about Jesus. And at that moment, she decided to do something that would completely turn her situation around for the better . . .

> *"If I just touch his clothes, I will be healed."*
> Mark 5:28 (NIV)

Your

FAITH TURN-AROUND POINT

Your faith doesn't need to be perfect. It just needs to reach out.

The streets were packed with people.

Everyone had heard about this Jesus who was performing miracles everywhere He went and preaching with such wisdom and authority that even the Pharisees took notice.

It would have been easy for this woman to think, *There's no way I can get to Jesus.*

Yet, her desperation fueled determination. She pushed past the obstacles, fear, doubt, and shame, and reached out — just for the edge of His robe.

Immediately, the bleeding ceased. She was completely healed!

But then Jesus stopped. He turned around. *"Who touched My robe?"* (Mark 5:30, NLT). The disciples were confused. *"Look at this crowd pressing around you. How can you ask, 'Who touched me?'"* (v. 31).

Jesus knew this wasn't any casual touch. It was faith in action.

The same Jesus — the One who healed her, restored her, and called her "daughter" — is the same Jesus who sees you today.

Trembling, the woman came forward, expecting a rebuke. She fell to her knees at Jesus' feet, admitting what she had done.

Full of grace and love, Jesus looked at her and said, *"Daughter, your faith has made you well. Go in peace. Your suffering is over"* (Mark 5:34, NLT).

In one moment, this woman wasn't only healed — she was restored.

You see, God's healing didn't stop at her suffering — He called her "daughter." That's significant because, for 12 years, she had been seen as unclean, an outcast, and unworthy.

But Jesus wanted her to know she was no longer defined by her suffering. Her identity was secure in and through Him.

She went from being unseen to known, from rejected to accepted. And that same Jesus — the One who healed her, restored her, and called her "daughter" — is the same Jesus who sees you today.

Your faith doesn't have to be perfect. It needs to reach out.

What's more, Jesus didn't even lay hands on her. Her faith was enough!

Maybe you've been carrying something — a sickness, a struggle, or a shame from your past. Maybe you've felt unseen, overlooked, or unworthy. Let me remind you that Jesus calls you His.

Like this woman, don't sit back and accept defeat.

Press through the doubt. Press through the fear. Press through whatever is holding you back. Then, receive the healing and restoration God has for you.

> **It's time for a turnaround. Jesus is near, and He has what you need.**

Your faith doesn't have to be perfect. It needs to reach out.

When you take that step toward Him, He will meet you with breakthrough.

Even now, your miracle is within reach!

But he was pierced for our transgressions, he was crushed for our iniquities; the punishment that brought us peace was on him, and by his wounds we are healed.

ISAIAH 53:5 (NIV)

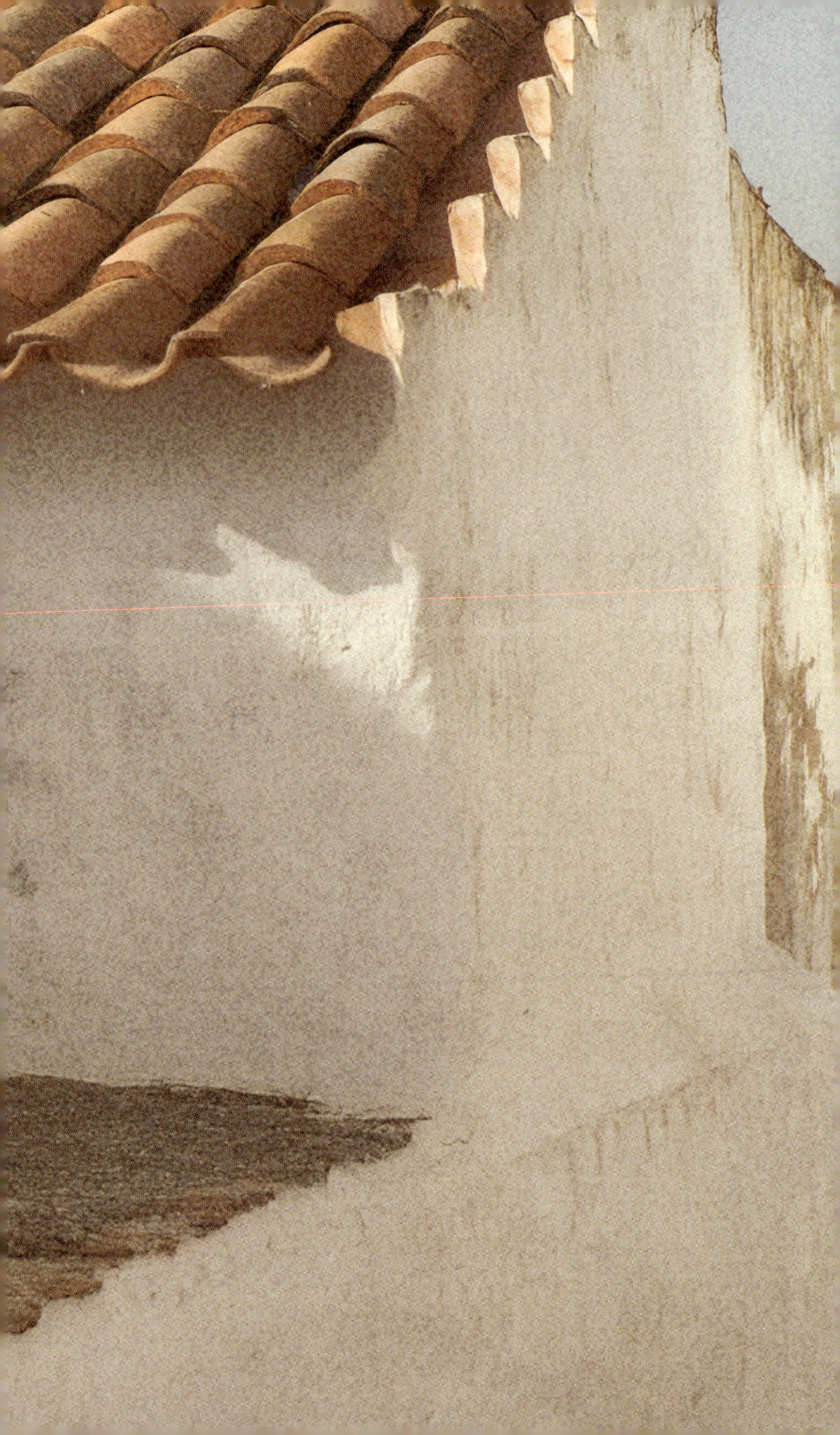

Chapter 8

BELIEF THAT BREAKS BARRIERS

Everyone was amazed and gave praise to God. They were filled with awe and said, "We have seen remarkable things today."

LUKE 5:26 (NIV)

The place was packed to overflowing. People had gathered from all over to hear Jesus teach in the intimate setting of a house. But in the crowd was a man who desperately needed a miracle — a paralyzed man who couldn't get to Jesus on his own.

Thankfully, he had four friends who refused to let obstacles stop them. They carried him to the house. And even when they saw the enormity of the crowd, they didn't turn back or get discouraged. They climbed onto the roof and tore a hole in it!

If they couldn't get through the door, they'd make a way through the ceiling. And right there in front of the crowd and Jesus Himself, they lowered their friend . . .

When Jesus saw their faith, he said, "Friend, your sins are forgiven."
Luke 5:20 (NIV)

Your FAITH TURN- AROUND POINT

Surround yourself with faith-filled people and refuse to give up.

The crowd must have been shocked.

Who would dare interrupt Jesus as he preached? Who would be so bold as to break this barrier, to rip a hole in a roof?

Jesus wasn't frustrated. He wasn't annoyed. He was *moved* by their faith.

Perhaps surprisingly, however, Jesus' first words weren't to heal the paralyzed man. He wanted to speak to his soul.

Jesus said, "*Your sins are forgiven*" (Luke 5:20, NIV). Some of the religious leaders were upset upon hearing these words. They thought to themselves, "*Who is this fellow who speaks blasphemy? Who can forgive sins but God alone?*" (v. 21).

Here's what happened next . . .

> *Jesus knew what they were thinking and asked, "Why are you thinking these things in your hearts? Which is easier: to say, 'Your sins are forgiven,' or to say, 'Get up and walk'? But I want you to know that the Son of Man has authority on earth to forgive sins." So he said to the paralyzed man, "I tell you, get up, take your mat and go home." Immediately he stood up in front of them, took what he had been lying on and went home praising God. Everyone was*

amazed and gave praise to God. They were filled with awe and said, "We have seen remarkable things today."
(Luke 5:22–26, NIV)

Jesus is still healing.
He's still restoring.
He's still speaking life over your situation.

Believe it!

Sometimes, we're so focused on our outward struggles that we don't realize God wants to do something deeper.

Maybe today, you feel stuck — like this paralyzed man. You want to move forward, but something is holding you back. Maybe it's fear, doubt, or past mistakes. Perhaps you have a physical ailment or disease that's limiting you.

Let me encourage you — Jesus is still healing. He's still restoring. He's still speaking life over your situation.

Maybe you need some "roof-breaking" friends . . .

People who will believe for you when you can't believe for yourself. Friends who will pray when you feel too weary.

Sometimes, we're so focused on our outward struggles that we don't realize God wants to do something deeper.

Friends who will remind you of God's promises when you're struggling to hold on.

Sometimes, our faith gets tired. The weight of waiting, the discouragement of delays, the frustration of unanswered prayers — they can each make us feel like we'll never get our breakthrough.

But here's the good news: You don't have to carry the weight alone.

Today, you may be on a stretcher. You're in a season where you don't have the strength to fight anymore. That's okay:

God wants to place people in your life to lift you up, intercede on your behalf, and help carry you into His presence.

What's more, God wants you to be that kind of friend for someone else! Perhaps there's someone around you who feels forgotten. Someone whose faith is wavering, who needs encouragement, who needs you to stand in the gap for them.

The friends in this story refused to let obstacles stop them. They saw the crowd; they saw the blocked entrance, but instead of giving up, they found another way.

Are you willing to press forward like that?

When you refuse to quit, when you push past the obstacles, when you surround yourself with faith-filled people — that's what sets your turnaround in motion.

Jesus sees your faith. And that faith is about to open doors, break barriers, *or even rip open some roofs* you never imagined!

Now that we know what we have — Jesus, this great High Priest with ready access to God — let's not let it slip through our fingers. We don't have a priest who is out of touch with our reality. He's been through weakness and testing, experienced it all — all but the sin. So let's walk right up to him and get what he is so ready to give. Take the mercy, accept the help.

HEBREWS 4:14–16 (MSG)

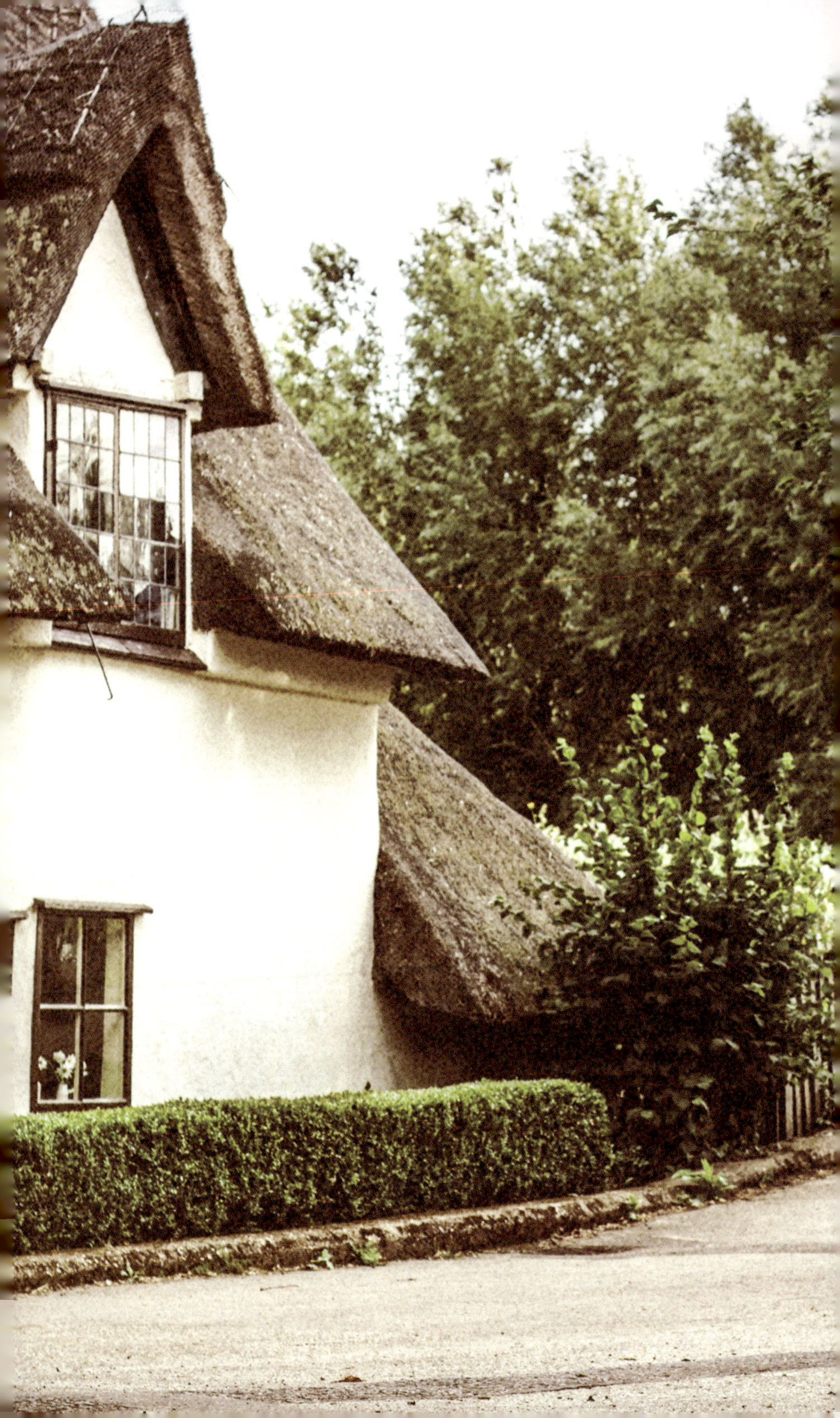

Chapter 9
GRACE IS GREATER

God saved you by his grace when you believed. And you can't take credit for this; it is a gift from God.

EPHESIANS 2:8 (NLT)

The Prodigal Son seemingly had everything — love, security, and a home with his father. But one day, he decided he wanted more. He asked for his inheritance early, packed his bags, and walked away from his father's house.

At first, life was good. He enjoyed everything the world had to offer. But when the money ran out and a famine hit the land, he found himself broke, alone, and desperate. He was so hungry that he took a job feeding pigs — something unthinkable for a Jewish man.

As he looked at the filthy, slop-covered food the pigs were eating, he realized even they were better off than him. That's when his turnaround began . . .

> "When he came to his senses, he said, 'How many of my father's hired servants have food to spare, and here I am starving to death! I will set out and go back to my father and say to him: Father, I have sinned against heaven and against you. I am no longer worthy to be called your son; make me like one of your hired servants.' So he got up and went to his father."
> Luke 15:17–20 (NIV)

Your

FAITH
TURN-
AROUND
POINT

The moment you turn toward God, He runs toward you.

Everything shifted when this son who had run away decided to return home. His circumstances may not have changed, but his heart had.

He started the long journey home, practicing his apology the whole way. He expected shame. He anticipated rejection. He hoped, *Maybe my father will at least let me work as a servant.*

What he didn't realize was that his father had never stopped looking for him.

As the son came down the road, the father saw him from a distance. And instead of waiting for him to arrive, instead of making him explain himself — his father ran to him.

He embraced him, kissed him, and before the son could even finish his rehearsed apology, the father called for his servants:

> **"Bring the best robe! Put a ring on his finger! Kill the fattened calf! My son was lost, but now he's found!"**

God isn't waiting to shame you. He's waiting to restore you!

Shame was replaced with celebration. The father didn't make his son earn his way back. He didn't say, "I told you so." He didn't condemn him. He welcomed him home.

Our Heavenly Father is no different. Even when we've messed up, even when we've walked away, He's still waiting with open arms.

> **The father didn't just restore the son — he showed us the heart of our Heavenly Father. That's what this story was always about — it's a picture of God's love for us.**

Maybe today, you feel far from God. Perhaps you've made some mistakes and think God won't welcome you back.

If so, it's not too late!

- **God's grace is greater than your worst mistakes.** No failure is too big for God's forgiveness.

- **God's grace is greater than your shame and regret.** The son expected rejection, but he

God doesn't hold your past against you, He restores you!

was met with love. God doesn't hold your past against you, He restores you!

- **God's grace is greater than any distance you could run.** No matter how far you've strayed or how alone you feel, you are never too far for His love to reach you.

- **God's grace is greater than your brokenness.** Grace isn't only for those who have it all together — it's for those who know they need Him.

- **God's grace is greater than feelings of unworthiness.** The son thought he wasn't worthy to be called a son, but the father called him beloved. God's grace reminds you that you are His, no matter what.

- **God's grace is greater than wasted opportunities.** The son squandered his inheritance, yet he was still given a place at the table. How is this possible? Because grace restores what was lost and gives you a new beginning.

- **God's grace is greater than the opinions of others.** The world may say you're unredeemable, but grace has the final word. When your Heavenly Father looks at you, He doesn't see a failure; He sees His fully forgiven and loved child.

Today, don't let guilt keep you from coming home. And if you know someone who is far from God, don't stop praying for them. Like the father in this story, keep looking for them to come home. Because when they do, there's going to be a celebration.

God's grace is greater, and the best is yet to come!

Draw near to God and He will draw near to you.

JAMES 4:8 (NKJV)

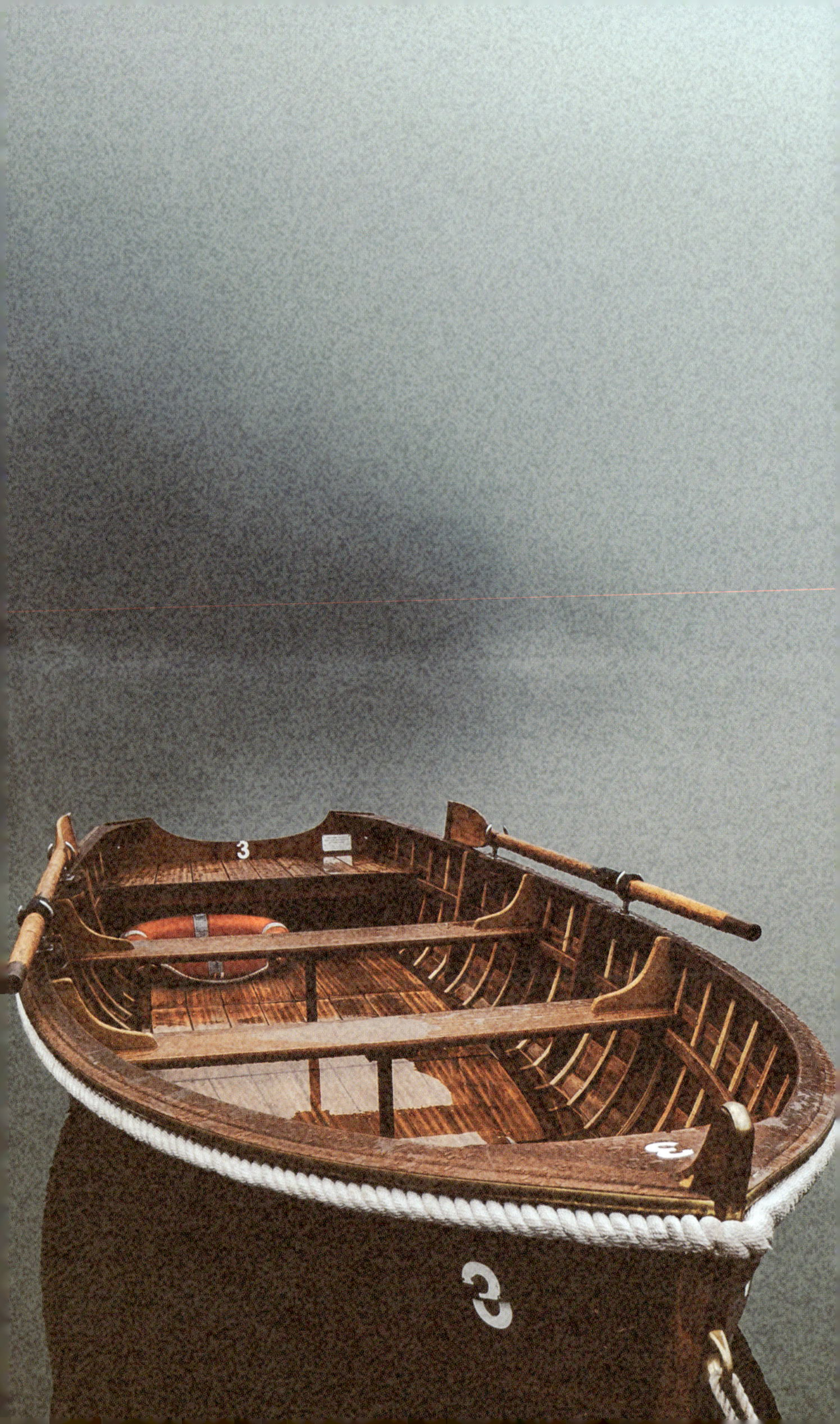

Chapter 10

A FAITH-FILLED FOCUS

"Come," he said. Then Peter got down out of the boat, walked on the water and came toward Jesus.

MATTHEW 14:29 (NIV)

A FAITH-FILLED FOCUS

It was a long day. Jesus had fed thousands with five loaves and two fish. As night fell, He told His disciples to get into a boat and go to the other side of the lake while He went up on a mountain to pray.

Out on the water, the wind started to rise. The disciples were struggling to keep control amid the crashing waves. Then, just before dawn, they saw something — or someone — walking toward them on the water.

Fear gripped their hearts. "It's a ghost!" they cried. But then they heard a familiar voice. *"Take courage! It is I. Don't be afraid"* (Matthew 14:27, NIV).

That's when Peter did something bold . . .

> *"Lord, if it's you," Peter replied, "tell me to come to you on the water." "Come," he said. Then Peter got down out of the boat, walked on the water and came toward Jesus.*
> Matthew 14:28–29 (NIV)

Your
FAITH TURN-AROUND POINT

Keep your eyes on Jesus. Faith flourishes when you focus on Him amidst the storm.

Peter did what no one else dared to do. He stepped out of the boat and started walking on the waves!

Think about what that must have felt like — to feel solid ground beneath your feet only for it to be liquid water in reality.

It was a miracle of supernatural proportions. And as Peter kept his eyes on Jesus, as he kept moving forward in faith, the miracle continued.

But then, as quickly as the miracle began, it ended.

Peter felt the wind. He looked again at the waves crashing and swirling beneath his feet. Fear took hold and he started to sink.

He cried out, *"Lord, save me!"* (v. 30).

Immediately, Jesus reached out His hand and caught him. "You of little faith, why did you doubt?" (v. 31).

> **Peter didn't sink because the storm was too strong — he sank because he let the storm become bigger in his eyes than Jesus.**

Jesus didn't say those words to rebuke Peter. He spoke to encourage him, to remind him that as long as he kept his eyes on *Him*, anything was possible.

> **Peter's mistake wasn't stepping out of the boat — it was taking his eyes off Jesus.**

And yet — Jesus didn't let him drown. The moment Peter called, Jesus reached out.

Maybe right now, you're in the middle of some winds and waves. You started strong in faith, but now the storm feels overwhelming.

- You took a step of faith in your career — trusting God for a new opportunity — but now the door has closed, and you don't see another one opening.

Like Peter, cry out to Jesus. He will reach for you, lift you up, and calm the storm.

- You believed for healing, stood on God's promises, and even saw some improvement — but now the symptoms are back, the doctor's report isn't good, and doubt is creeping in.

- You've been praying for a loved one to turn back to God, but instead, it seems like they're drifting further away.

- You thought a relationship would last, but now you're facing betrayal, heartbreak, or divorce. You wonder how to move forward.

- You stepped into ministry, believing God was calling you to make an impact — but now, discouragement, setbacks, and lack of support have left you questioning if you even heard Him right.

Remember, Peter didn't sink because the storm was too strong — he sank because he let the storm become bigger in his eyes than Jesus.

That's what fear does. It takes our eyes off Jesus and magnifies the problem.

Fear makes the storm seem more powerful than the Savior. But don't focus on the storm. As long as you keep your eyes on Jesus, you'll rise above the waves.

Fear may try to pull you under. Doubt will try to make you sink. But like Peter, cry out to Jesus. He will reach for you, lift you up, and calm the storm.

The same Savior who made the water as solid as the ground beneath your feet is walking with you right now.

Therefore, since we are surrounded by such a great cloud of witnesses, let us throw off everything that hinders and the sin that so easily entangles. And let us run with perseverance the race marked out for us, fixing our eyes on Jesus, the pioneer and perfecter of faith. For the joy set before him he endured the cross, scorning its shame, and sat down at the right hand of the throne of God. Consider him who endured such opposition from sinners, so that you will not grow weary and lose heart.

HEBREWS 12:1-3 (NIV)

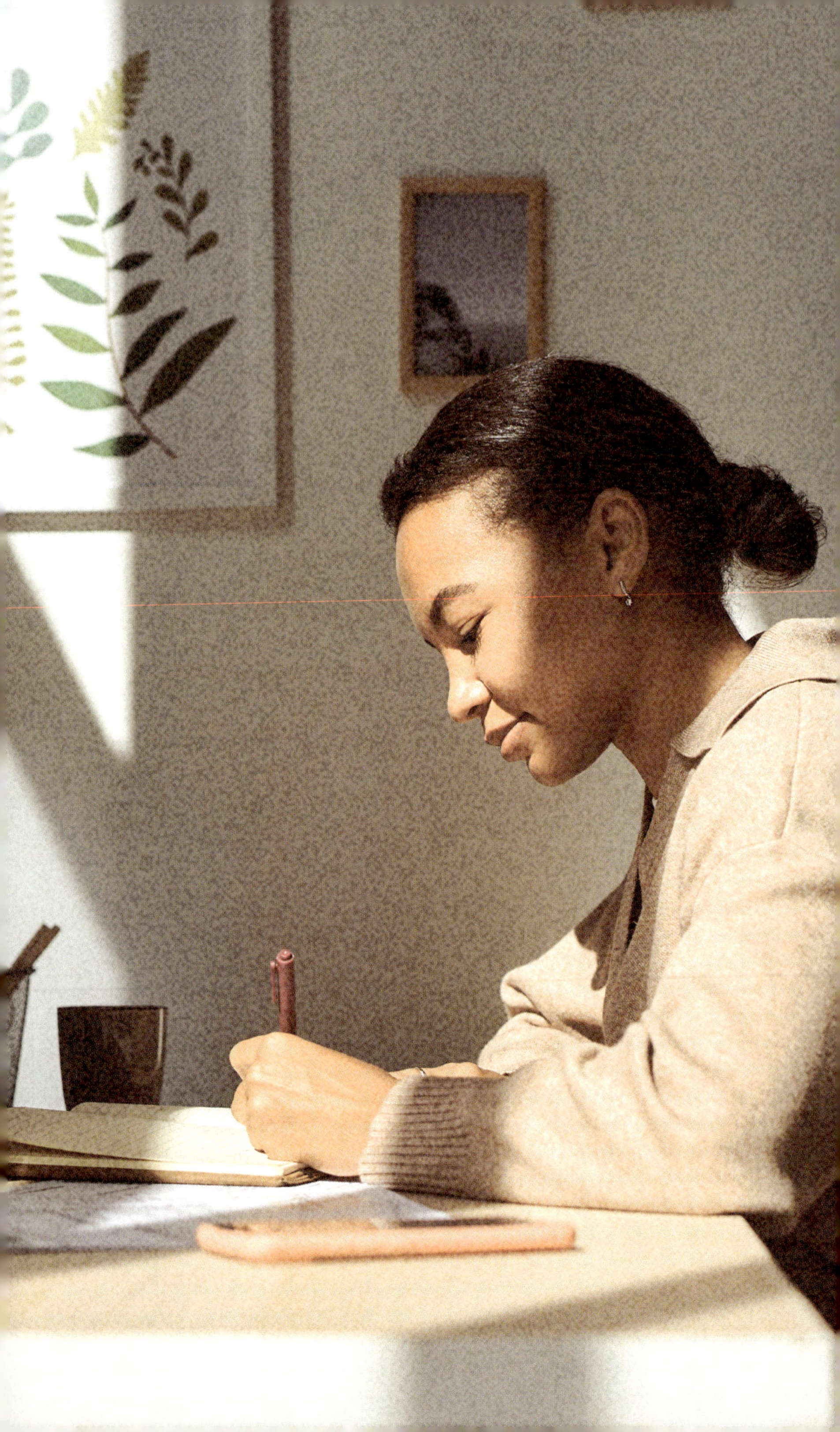

Chapter 11

RETURN AND REJOICE

Let us come into his presence with thanksgiving; let us make a joyful noise to him with songs of praise!

PSALM 95:2 (ESV)

Ten men stood at a distance, outcasts because of their disease. They had leprosy — an incurable condition that caused physical pain and social rejection.

When they saw Jesus, they cried out, *"Jesus, Master, have pity on us!"* (Luke 17:13, NIV).

Perhaps surprisingly, Jesus didn't touch them. He didn't heal them on the spot. He said, *"Go, show yourselves to the priests"* (v. 14). At that moment, they had a choice — stay where they were or respond in faith . . .

> *One of them, when he saw he was healed, came back, praising God in a loud voice. He threw himself at Jesus' feet and thanked him — and he was a Samaritan.*
> Luke 17:15–16 (NIV)

Your FAITH TURN-AROUND POINT

Don't only celebrate the gift but also thank the *Giver* and let gratitude deepen your faith.

The nine lepers obeyed Jesus' command. As they walked in faith, they were healed. Their skin, once covered in disease, was restored. Their lives were forever changed!

But something was missing.

Instead of returning to Jesus, they kept going. They had received what they wanted — a clean bill of health, a second chance at life — but they moved forward without looking back.

They were healed, yet they missed the Healer. Except for the one.

Scripture says, *"When he saw he was healed, came back, praising God with a loud voice"* (v. 15).

This story teaches us something powerful:

Gratitude is an act of faith.

The one who returned wasn't just thankful for his healing — he was thankful for Jesus. He didn't only receive the miracle and move on; he returned to rejoice.

> **When you live with gratitude, you shift your focus from the gift to the Giver. You remind yourself that God isn't good because He blesses you — He blesses you because *He* is good.**

Because of that, he received something more than physical healing — he received spiritual wholeness.

Jesus said to him, *"Rise and go; your faith has made you well"* (v. 19).

Maybe today, God has been answering prayers in your life. Perhaps you've seen doors open, provision come through, protection over your family, or peace settle in where fear used to be.

> **Are you pausing to thank God? Or are you so focused on the next thing that you forgot to praise Him for what He's already done?**

The other nine lepers were healed, but they never returned to the Healer. They were focused on moving forward with

God isn't good because He blesses you — He blesses you because *He* is good.

their newfound freedom, but they missed the opportunity to go deeper with Jesus.

We can do the same thing sometimes. We can pray, ask, and believe — and when the breakthrough comes, we celebrate for a moment and then move on to the next need.

When you live with gratitude, however, you shift your focus from the gift to the Giver. You remind yourself that God isn't good because He blesses you — He blesses you because *He* is good.

- **When a prayer is answered, you don't stop seeking God — you draw even closer to Him.** You don't just rejoice in the breakthrough; you rejoice in the One who made it possible.

- **When life is going well, you don't take credit — you give God the glory.** You acknowledge that your open doors and opportunities are a result of His favor, not just your efforts.

- **When you're in a difficult season, you still praise God** — not just for what He's done but for who He is. You choose gratitude, trusting that He is working even when you don't see it.

- **When you experience healing, you don't just celebrate the recovery — you worship the Healer.** You focus on His power, faithfulness, and love, not only the relief from the pain or diagnosis.

- **When someone helps you in a time of need, you don't just thank them — you thank God for putting the right people in your life.** You see His hand in the relationships He's given you.

Today, let gratitude change your perspective, deepen your faith, and position you for greater things!

And whatever you do, whether in word or deed, do it all in the name of the Lord Jesus, giving thanks to God the Father through him.

COLOSSIANS 3:17 (NIV)

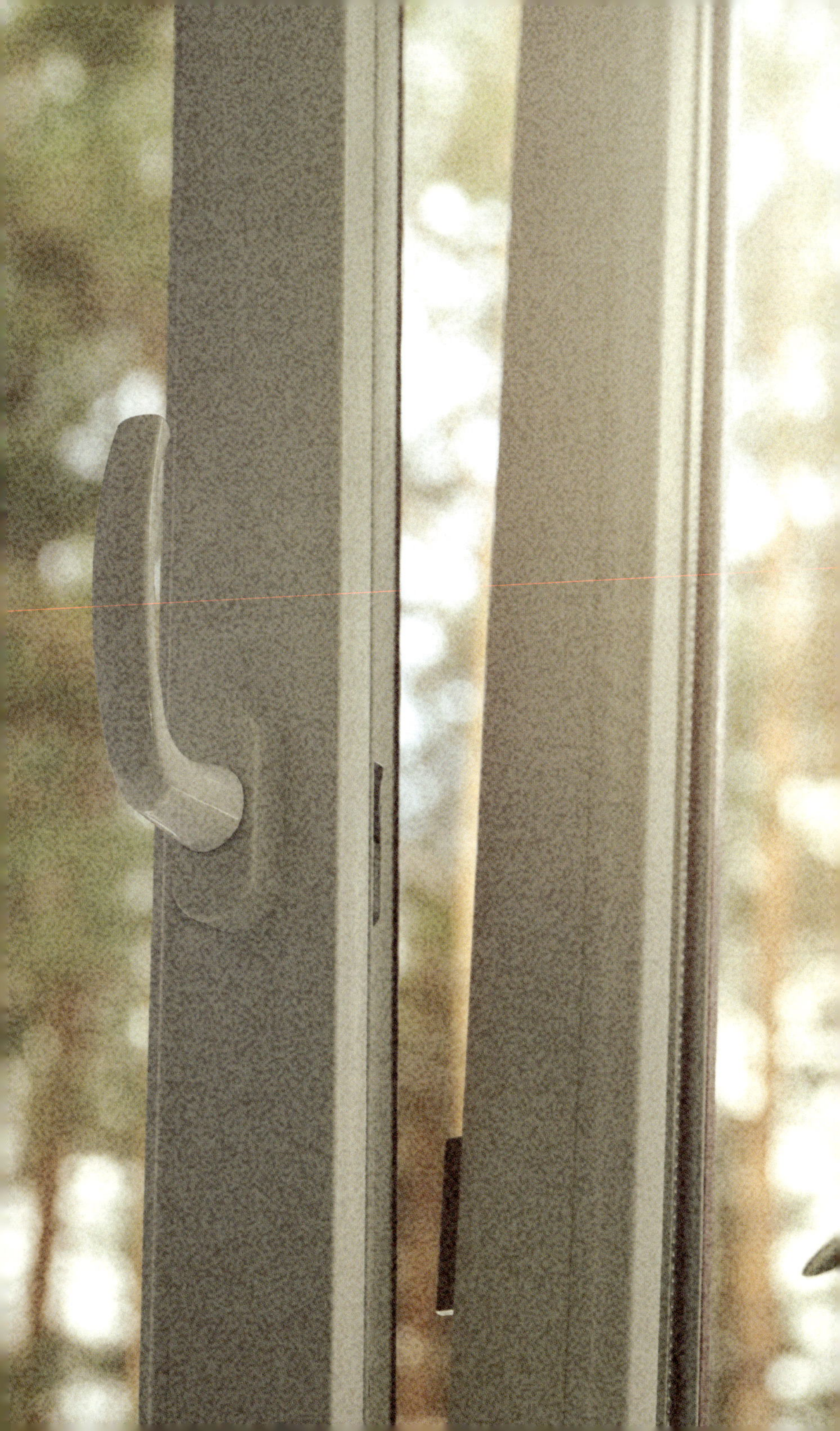

# Chapter 12

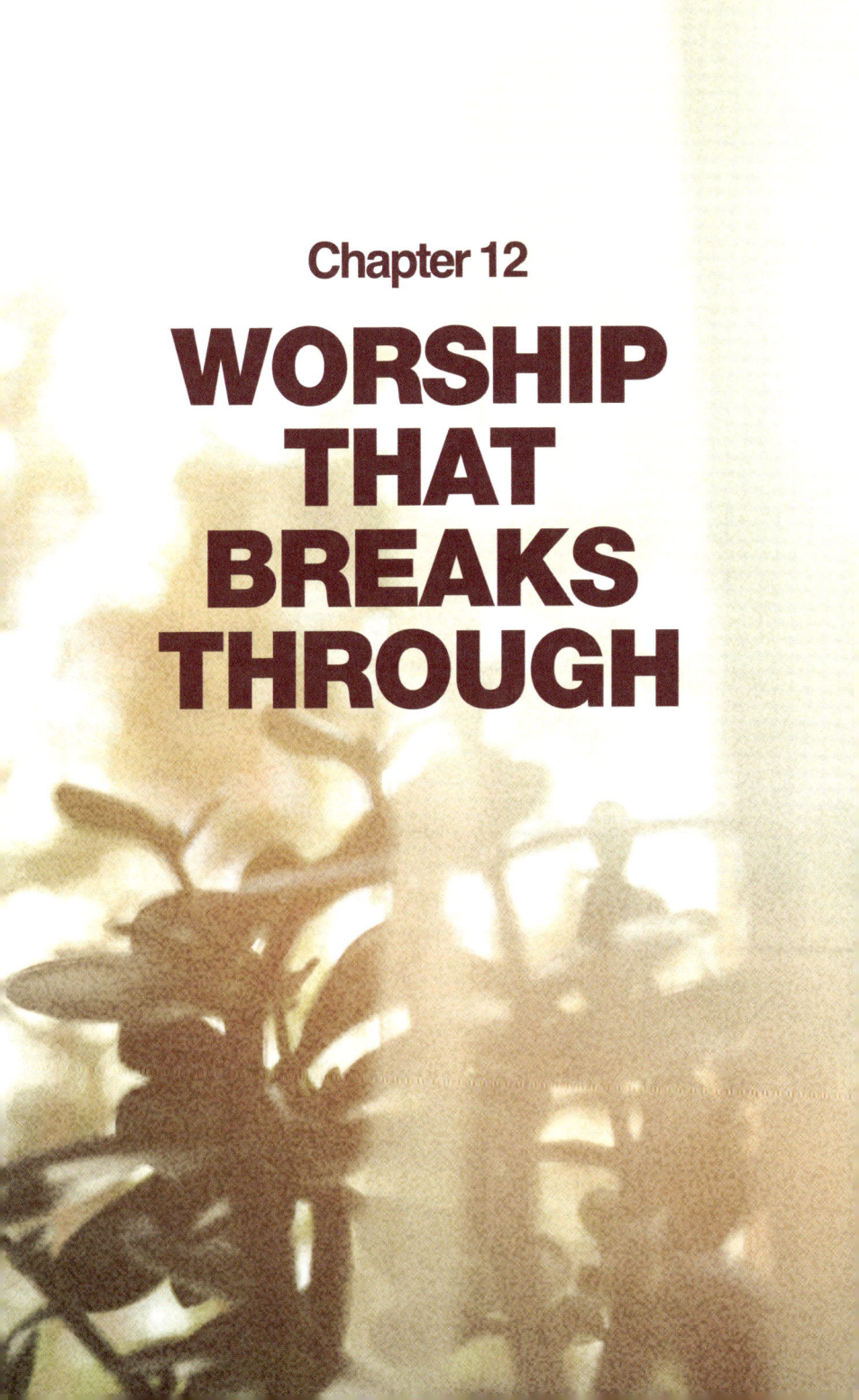

WORSHIP THAT BREAKS THROUGH

Suddenly there was such a violent earthquake that the foundations of the prison were shaken. At once all the prison doors flew open, and everyone's chains came loose.

ACTS 16:26 (NIV)

P aul and Silas had been preaching the Gospel, setting people free, and doing the work of God. But instead of being celebrated, they were attacked.

They were falsely accused, beaten with rods, and thrown into the deepest part of a Roman prison. Locked in stocks, their bodies bruised and bleeding — their future looked uncertain.

In the natural, they had every reason to be discouraged. But instead of complaining, instead of questioning God, they made a decision that changed everything . . .

> *About midnight Paul and Silas were praying and singing hymns to God, and the other prisoners were listening to them.*
> Acts 16:25 (NIV)

Your FAITH TURN-AROUND POINT

Worship in your midnight moment — your praise is paving the way for breakthrough!

Paul and Silas didn't wait until they were free to worship — they worshiped while they were still in chains. And the moment they did, their prison turned into a place of praise and breakthrough.

Suddenly, an earthquake shook the prison. The doors flew open, the chains fell off, and every prisoner was set free!

The jailer woke up, thinking all the prisoners had escaped. He was about to take his own life, but Paul called out, *"Don't harm yourself! We are all here!"* (Acts 16:28, NIV).

The jailer ran in, fell to his knees, and asked, *"Sirs, what must I do to be saved?"* (v. 30). That very night, he and his entire family gave their lives to Jesus.

What started as a night of suffering became a night of salvation.

God didn't just deliver Paul and Silas — He used their praise to bring freedom to an entire household.

Maybe right now, you feel trapped. You're in a tough situation, and you don't see a way out.

> **Midnight isn't the end — it's the setup for your miracle. Your worship isn't pointless — it's preparing the way for your breakthrough!**

The midnight moments of life — the times when everything feels dark, the answers seem far away, and the weight of uncertainty is heavy — are where your faith is tested the most.

You can choose to despair and doubt God's plan. Or you can choose to worship.

Worship is about more than singing a song — it's about posturing your heart in faith.

> **Worship is declaring God's goodness even when circumstances say otherwise. It's lifting your hands in surrender when fear tries to paralyze you.**

Worship can look like praying with expectation, even when you haven't seen the answer. It can be speaking life over

When you worship in your midnight moment, Heaven moves, chains break, and victory begins!

your situation instead of agreeing with discouragement. It can be thanking God in advance for what He's about to do.

Maybe worship for you today is simply saying, "God, I trust You." Maybe it's filling your home with praise music or taking a moment to read Scripture aloud.

No matter what your worship looks like, it shifts your focus from the storm to the Savior. And when you worship in your midnight moment, Heaven moves, chains break, and victory begins!

> **Paul and Silas didn't praise God because of their situation — they praised Him despite it. And when they did, their chains broke, their prison doors opened, and their testimony brought others to Jesus.**

Always remember, your praise is your weapon. Instead of focusing on the problem, start worshiping the One who holds the solution.

Choose to see midnight not as the end but as the setup for your breakthrough.

Your chains are about to break. Your prison doors are about to swing open. And your faith will become the testimony that leads others to Jesus!

Like Paul and Silas, your breakthrough and victory are already in motion!

LORD, you are my God; I will exalt you and praise your name, for in perfect faithfulness you have done wonderful things, things planned long ago.

ISAIAH 25:1 (NIV)

Scriptures to Encourage You

"So do not fear, for I am with you; do not be dismayed, for I am your God. I will strengthen you and help you; I will uphold you with my righteous right hand."
Isaiah 41:10 (NIV)

And God is able to bless you abundantly, so that in all things at all times, having all that you need, you will abound in every good work.
2 Corinthians 9:8 (NIV)

The righteous cry out, and the Lord hears them; he delivers them from all their troubles.
Psalm 34:17 (NIV)

"The LORD himself goes before you and will be with you; he will never leave you nor forsake you. Do not be afraid; do not be discouraged."
Deuteronomy 31:8 (NIV)

No, in all these things we are more than conquerors through him who loved us.
Romans 8:37 (NIV)

Cast your cares on the Lord and he will sustain you; he will never let the righteous be shaken.
Psalm 55:22 (NIV)

And my God will meet all your needs according to the riches of his glory in Christ Jesus.
Philippians 4:19 (NIV)

"Have I not commanded you? Be strong and courageous. Do not be afraid; do not be discouraged, for the Lord your God will be with you wherever you go."
Joshua 1:9 (NIV)

My help comes from the Lord, the Maker of heaven and earth.
Psalm 121:2 (NIV)

"See, I am doing a new thing! Now it springs up; do you not perceive it? I am making a way in the wilderness and streams in the wasteland."
Isaiah 43:19 (NIV)

God is our refuge and strength, an ever-present help in trouble.
Psalm 46:1 (NIV)

The Lord is good, a refuge in times of trouble. He cares for those who trust in him.
Nahum 1:7 (NIV)

You will keep in perfect peace those whose minds are steadfast, because they trust in you. Trust in the Lord forever, for the Lord, the Lord himself, is the Rock eternal.
Isaiah 26:3–4 (NIV)

May the God of hope fill you with all joy and peace as you trust in him, so that you may overflow with hope by the power of the Holy Spirit.
Romans 15:13 (NIV)

"I have told you these things, so that in me you may have peace. In this world you will have trouble. But take heart! I have overcome the world."
John 16:33 (NIV)

For the Spirit God gave us does not make us timid, but gives us power, love and self-discipline.
2 Timothy 1:7 (NIV)

Let us hold unswervingly to the hope we profess, for he who promised is faithful.
Hebrews 10:23 (NIV)

"Because of the Lord's great love we are not consumed, for his compassions never fail. They are new every morning; great is your faithfulness."
Lamentations 3:22–23 (NIV)

Therefore, my dear brothers and sisters, stand firm. Let nothing move you. Always give yourselves fully to the work of the Lord, because you know that your labor in the Lord is not in vain.
1 Corinthians 15:58 (NIV)

On that day they will say to Jerusalem, "Do not fear, Zion; do not let your hands hang limp. The LORD your God is with you, the Mighty Warrior who saves. He will take great delight in you; in his love he will no longer rebuke you, but will rejoice over you with singing."
Zephaniah 3:16–17 (NIV)

ABOUT JOEL OSTEEN MINISTRIES

Joel Osteen Ministries, rooted in Houston, Texas, is an extension of the legacy built by John and Dodie Osteen, who founded Lakewood Church in 1959. Originally meeting in a modest feed store, Lakewood has grown into one of the largest congregations in the U.S., attracting people from all walks of life. John Osteen's leadership touched millions through his television ministry, which reached over 100 countries, and his influence as a pastor's pastor. His wife, Dodie, also played a key role, especially with her testimony of miraculous healing from cancer, which has inspired countless people.

When John passed away in 1999, his son Joel stepped into leadership, despite his background in television production. Joel's transition into senior pastor marked a new era for Lakewood, with the church's global influence expanding significantly. Under Joel's leadership, Lakewood's outreach grew, broadcasting to over 200 million households, and the church became a beacon of hope for millions seeking encouragement and inspiration.

Joel's wife, Victoria, serves alongside him, contributing to the church's leadership and vision. Their daughter, Alexandra, continues the family tradition, leading worship and contributing to Lakewood Music. With a focus on uplifting messages and practical teachings, Joel Osteen Ministries aims to reach new generations, inspiring people worldwide to rise above their challenges and live their best life through faith, hope, and love.

Stay encouraged *and* inspired all through the week.

Download the Joel Osteen Daily Podcast *and* subscribe now *on* YouTube to get the latest videos.

For a full listing, visit **JoelOsteen.com/How-To-Watch**.

SiriusXM · Apple Podcasts · Spotify · YouTube · ROKU

Stay connected, *be* blessed.

Get more from Joel & Victoria Osteen

It's time to step into the life of victory and favor that God has planned for you! Featuring new messages from Joel & Victoria Osteen, their free daily devotional, and inspiring articles, hope is always at your fingertips with the free Joel Osteen app and online at JoelOsteen.com.

Get the app and visit us today at JoelOsteen.com.

Download on the App Store

GET IT ON Google Play

JOEL OSTEEN MINISTRIES

CONNECT WITH US